W9-CBQ-058

FREDERICK DOUGLASS

FIGHTER AGAINST SLAVERY

Famous
African Americans

Patricia and
Fredrick McKissack

Enslow Elementary
an imprint of
Enslow Publishers, Inc.

40 Industrial Road
Box 398
Berkeley Heights, NJ 07922
USA
http://www.enslow.com

To Blake

Enslow Elementary, an imprint of Enslow Publishers, Inc.

Enslow Elementary® is a registered trademark of Enslow Publishers, Inc.

Revised edition of *Frederick Douglass: Leader Against Slavery* © 1991

Library of Congress Cataloging-in-Publication Data

McKissack, Pat, 1944-
  Frederick Douglass : fighter against slavery / Patricia and Fredrick McKissack.
    p. cm.
  Previously published: Berkeley Heights, NJ : Enslow Pub., c2002.
  Summary: "A simple biography about Frederick Douglass, Jr. for early readers"—Provided by publisher.
  Includes index.
  ISBN 978-0-7660-4098-4
  1. Douglass, Frederick, 1818-1895—Juvenile literature.
  2. Abolitionists—United States—Biography—Juvenile literature.
  3. African-American abolitionists—Biography—Juvenile literature.
  4. Antislavery movements—United States—History—19th century—Juvenile literature. I. McKissack, Fredrick. II. Title.
  E449.D75M378 2013
  973.8092—dc23
  [B]

                    2012019031

Future editions:
Paperback ISBN 978-1-4644-0196-1
ePUB ISBN 978-1-4645-1109-7
PDF ISBN 978-1-4646-1109-4

Printed in the United States of America

082012 Lake Book Manufacturing, Inc., Melrose Park, IL

10 9 8 7 6 5 4 3 2 1

To Our Readers: We have done our best to make sure all Internet Addresses in this book were active and appropriate when we went to press. However, the author and the publisher have no control over and assume no liability for the material available on those Internet sites or on other Web sites they may link to. Any comments or suggestions can be sent by e-mail to comments@enslow.com or to the address on the back cover.

Every effort has been made to locate all copyright holders of material used in this book. If any errors or omissions have occurred, corrections will be made in future editions of this book.

♻ Enslow Publishers, Inc., is committed to printing our books on recycled paper. The paper in every book contains 10% to 30% post-consumer waste (PCW). The cover board on the outside of each book contains 100% PCW. Our goal is to do our part to help young people and the environment too!

Photo Credits: Anna Murray Douglass, My Mother As I Recall Her © 1900, frontispiece, p. 14; Library of Congress, pp. 3, 4, 13, 16, 20; My Bondage and My Freedom: Part I- Life as a Slave, Part II- Life as a Freeman © 1855, frontispiece, p. 1.

Illustration Credits: Ned O., pp. 7, 8, 10.

Cover Photo: My Bondage and My Freedom: Part I- Life as a Slave, Part II- Life as a Freeman © 1855, frontispiece.

Words in bold type are explained in Words to Know on page 22.

Series Consultant:
Russell Adams, PhD
Emeritus Professor
Afro-American Studies
Howard University

CONTENTS

Frederick Douglass was born a slave. When he grew up, he became a powerful voice against slavery.

CHAPTER 1
ALONE!

. . . .

Harriet Bailey was a **slave**. All her children were slaves, too. On (or near) Valentine's Day in 1817 or 1818, Harriet gave birth to a son. She named him Frederick Augustus Washington Bailey.

When the baby was one week old, Harriet was ordered back to work. But Frederick wasn't left alone. He was sent to live with his Grandmama Betsey and Grandpa Isaac.

Little Fred didn't see his mother very much. She worked far away. Fred was happy until he was about eight years old.

At that time Grandmama Betsey took him to the main **plantation**, in Tuckahoe, Maryland. She had been told to leave him there. Why, why? he cried.

The boy didn't understand slavery. Slaves had to do what their **masters** said.

The cook took care of all the children at the main plantation. She was a slave, too. Still, she beat young Fred when he cried.

One day the cook was going to beat Fred. But Harriet came in. "Never hit my child again," the angry mother said. The cook ran out of the room.

Harriet hugged her son. She fed him. She sang to him. Then it was time for her to go. Harriet had to do what her master said.

Fred never saw his mother again. Harriet died soon after that visit.

Fred was alone.

Fred's mother was very upset when she saw the cook hurting her son.

Fred learned how to read from his master's wife. Most slaves did not know how to read.

CHAPTER 2
NEVER!

Fred lived at the main plantation for a year. The cook beat him almost every day.

Then Fred was sent to be a house slave for Sophia and Hugh Auld.

Sophia Auld was a kind woman. She taught her son and Fred how to read and write.

Then one day Fred read for Hugh Auld. Mr. Auld was very, very angry. "Never teach a slave to read," said Mr. Auld. "He won't want to stay a slave."

Mrs. Auld stopped teaching Fred how to read. But Fred didn't stop reading.

When Fred was sixteen, he was sent back to the main plantation in Tuckahoe. Thomas Auld was his master.

Fred wouldn't act like a slave. So Auld sent him to a **slave-breaker**. Fred was made to work from morning

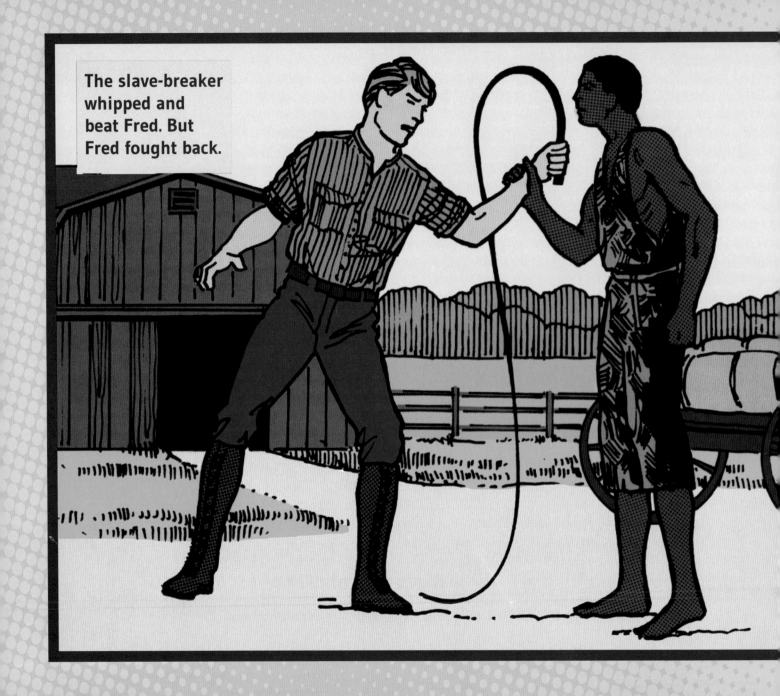

The slave-breaker whipped and beat Fred. But Fred fought back.

until night. All he had to do was act like a slave. But Fred said, "Never!" He stayed with the slave-breaker for almost a year.

One day Fred fought back. He stopped the slave-breaker from beating him. Auld and the slave-breaker had tried to make Fred a willing slave. Now they knew that it would never work.

Thomas Auld sent Frederick back to Hugh and Sophia. By that time, Fred knew that he was going to run away.

CHAPTER 3
RUN!

. . . .

It was 1838. Frederick was eighteen years old and very good-looking.

He met Anna, a free black woman who lived in Baltimore, Maryland. He loved Anna and wanted to marry her. But Frederick wouldn't ask—not until he was free, too.

Freedom was always on his mind. He wanted to run. Run! Run! His friends said wait. He needed a plan.

After many months of planning, Frederick was ready to run. At last the day came. Dressed as a free sailor, he rode a train to Delaware. Blacks who were not slaves had to carry special papers—called **free papers**—all the time. Frederick's free papers belonged to a friend. If anyone checked, he would be in trouble. But no one checked closely.

This sheet music shows Frederick Douglass as he ran from Maryland to freedom.

Frederick's wife Anna was born free. She helped Frederick to be free also.

Then, from Delaware, Frederick took a boat to Philadelphia. Run, Fred, run! From Philadelphia, he went to New York. Run, Fred, run!

On September 4, 1838, Frederick was in a **free state**. He changed his name to Frederick Augustus Douglass. He hoped slave catchers would not find him.

Right away, he sent for Anna. They were married in New York. Soon, the happy couple moved to New Bedford, Massachusetts. Frederick got a job working on ships.

Soon he joined the **abolitionists**. These were people who wanted to end slavery. Frederick spoke out against slavery all over the North. He even wrote his own life story.

Then he had to run again. **Slave hunters** would be coming to take him back to his master. Frederick said good-bye to his family and hurried to England.

Two years later, on December 5, 1846, Frederick was truly freed. Friends had bought his freedom. He came back to the United States in 1847 with his own free papers. He never had to run again.

Everywhere he went, Frederick spoke out against slavery. The North Star was his anti-slavery newspaper.

Frederick founded the North Star in December 1847.

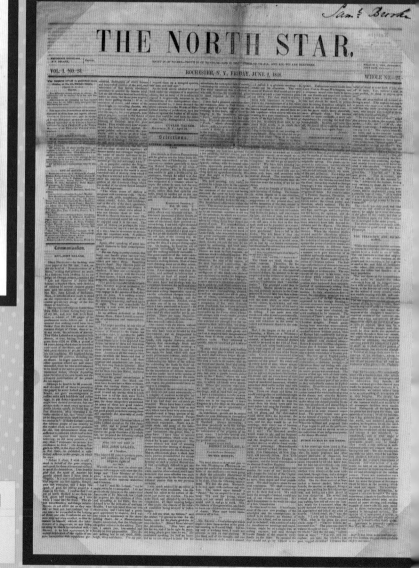

CHAPTER 4
FREEDOM!

. . . .

Frederick Douglass was a free man. But what about all those who were still slaves? He believed all people should be free. That would be his life's work.

The Douglasses moved to Rochester, New York. There, Frederick started the *North Star,* a weekly newspaper. The North Star was the light in the sky that **runaways** followed to freedom.

Abraham Lincoln was elected **president** of the United States in November 1860. South Carolina said it was no longer a part of the United States in December 1860. Other states in the South soon followed. The **Civil War** began in April 1861.

In 1863 Lincoln freed the slaves. Douglass wept when he heard the news. "What [Lincoln] has done is to [get rid of] a terrible evil that has [had hold of] this country. . . ."

Douglass met with President Lincoln in the **White House**. Douglass asked that black men be allowed to join the North's army. They had the right to fight for freedom.

Two of Douglass's sons were among the first black men to join the **Union Army**. Other black men followed. The African-American soldiers won many medals for **bravery** during the war.

Later Douglass pushed for equal pay for soldiers. "Black and white soldiers die the same," he said. "They should be paid the same." At last, both black and white soldiers were paid the same.

The war ended in 1865. President Lincoln was killed soon afterward. Douglass was very sad. He said, "It is a dark time for us all."

CHAPTER 5
HERO!

. . . .

When the Civil War ended, Frederick Douglass was called a hero. He had not been a soldier. But he had been fighting to end slavery for so long.

Some people thought Douglass's work was over. Instead, he tried new things. For a while he was president of a bank. And he also worked for women's rights.

Finally, the Douglasses closed the *North Star* and moved to **Washington, D.C.** President Rutherford B. Hayes had asked Douglass to be the **marshal of the District of Columbia**. In later years, he was chosen by other presidents to serve the **government**, too.

The Douglass home was called Cedar Hill. It was a happy place. People came to visit all the time. Anna always made their house a fun place. Their children were grown up. They had children of their own. It was full of happy

Frederick Douglass met with President Lincoln. In later years, Frederick still stood up for freedom and equal rights for all.

sounds and good smells. Frederick was never too busy to hug his grandchildren. Family was always very important to him.

Anna died after being ill. Once more Frederick was alone. He had never liked being alone. Soon he married a second time. Many people felt he should not have married again. But he was happy.

Frederick was not happy about the way things were changing. By the 1890s, unfair laws were being passed. Black people were losing their rights. Frederick Douglass was old and tired. But he still spoke up for freedom and justice. He always would.

He spoke to a large group in Washington, D.C., on February 20, 1895. Later that evening, Frederick Douglass died. A great American hero was gone.

Frederick will always be remembered as an abolitionist. He had been a slave. But he could never understand how one person could own another.

In a speech he gave one Fourth of July, he said, "There is no way a nation can call itself free and accept slavery." We know now that his words are true.

Words to Know

abolitionist—A person who wanted to end (abolish) slavery in the United States.

bravery—An act that shows courage. Standing up to fear.

Civil War—A war fought within one country. In the United States, the Civil War was fought between states in the North and the South from 1861 to 1865.

freedom—The power to make your own choices and decisions.

free papers—Papers showing that a person was not owned.

free state—A state that did not allow slavery.

government—A group that runs a country.

marshal of the District of Columbia—A law officer of the capital of the United States of America.

master—A ruler or a person who controls another. Someone who owns slaves is called a master.

plantation—A very large farm.

president—The leader of a country or group.

runaway—A slave who ran away to the North, where he or she could live in freedom.

slave—A person who is owned by another. That person can be bought or sold.

slave-breaker—Someone hired to beat slaves and teach them to obey or fear a master.

slave hunter—Someone who, for money, looked for runaway slaves and took them back to their masters.

Union Army—The army that fought for the North in the Civil War.

Washington, D.C.—The city where the United States government is located. D.C. stands for District Columbia.

White House—The house where the president of the United States lives.

LEARN MORE

BOOKS

Cline-Ransome, Lesa. *Words Set Me Free: The Story of Young Frederick Douglass.* New York: Simon & Schuster, 2012.

McLoone, Margo. *Frederick Douglass.* Danbury, Conn.: Children's Press, 2006.

Trumbauer, Lisa. *Let's Meet Frederick Douglass.* New York: Chelsea Clubhouse, 2003.

WEB SITES

Frederick Douglass National Historic Site: Photos and Multimedia
<http://www.nps.gov/frdo/photosmultimedia/photogallery.htm>

Garden of Praise: Frederick Douglass
<http://gardenofpraise.com/ibdfdoug.htm>

INDEX

J B DOUGLASS
McKissack, Pat
Frederick Douglass :
    fighter against slavery

R0120038799   PTREE